XY - B1
MPH 12/82

XY - B1
MPH 12/82

**BURMA
THE
GOLDEN**

BURMA THE GOLDEN

Designed and photographed by Günter Pfannmüller·Written by Wilhelm Klein

First Edition
Published by Apa Productions (hk) Ltd
for The Bookseller Co., Ltd.
Bangkok

Burma The Golden
First Edition 1982
ISBN 9971-925-25-7
© 1982 by Apa Productions (HK) Ltd

Printed in Singapore by Tien Wah Press (Pte) Ltd

Dedicated
to the People
of Burma

Myths are humanity's earliest answers to the mysteries of life. Burma is enveloped in myth like a cocoon. Within the myth lies dormant a beautiful butterfly whose myriad manifestations defy description.

It was our intention to catch in word and picture some of the many facets this country reveals to the inquiring mind, to the person who cuts through the cocoon to see beyond the mere facts of everyday life. For years we have visited Burma, on and off, trying to reduce the mythical into rational bits and pieces. We have sought to define the essence of Burma and to share with others the charm and enchantment that is at once overwhelming and others worldly.

One of the key components is the uniquely Burmese form of Buddhism. An all-pervasive way of life, it distinguishes the people of the Irrawaddy valley from most other inhabitants of Southeast Asia. Ethereal realms and fables of Theravada Buddhism have merged with ancient animistic nat-worship. The mind boggles with fairy-tale visions; incredibly, Burma's idyllic landscape is equal to the imagination. It is dotted everywhere with remarkable stupas, temples and monasteries.

In sharp contrast to this living fantasy, the Burmese people, while believing in doctrines formulated 25 centuries ago, live under a modern secular socialist constitution which somehow tries to reconcile two diametrically opposed philosophies. The government strives to answer the everyday material needs of the populace without blocking the *nibbanic* option — the belief in Buddhist deliverance which historically has been the moving factor in the country's development.

Indeed, the pious Buddhist sees earthly attainment as a waste of energy. For him, this lifetime is only one of many plightful transient existences in which he can do naught but refine his karma. One day, after innumerable rebirths, this might lead him to *nibbana* (nirvana). This Buddhist belief is a myth in the eyes of most Westerners. It clashes with the modern view that because this life is the only known quantity, happiness should be sought now, through rational and science-oriented living. Buddhists refute this with their own brand of science; they say the main ingredient of life will always be suffering.

While we were trying to document at least fractions of this basic contradiction underlying the reality of modern Burma, we realized that we had to penetrate the country on different levels. A horizontal study would catch Burma's geography, its visual truth; a vertical view would cover the historic development of the nation, its racial diversity, its religious expressions, and the artistic vestiges of generations long since past. Fortunately, Burma's showplaces of history are dispersed over the whole country. The custom of Burmese kings to periodically shift their capitals, and the choice of regions where diverse tribes have settled, gave us the opportunity to chronologically weave geographical sights with historical and philosophical facts.

And so we set out to unravel Burma's myths. But the more we tried to do so, the more snarled in those myths we became. One typically unreal Burmese night, we sat atop the U Min Kyaukse Pagoda overlooking Sagaing, listening to *pongyis* (monks), chanting from their Pali scriptures in a monotone sing-song. All at once we realized that the myth surrounding this ancient land cannot be untangled — that to try to demythify what has grown for millennia is like watching sand vanish between your fingers. Just when you think you've finally got hold of it, you see there is nothing worthwhile left to describe, nothing remaining that is constant.

We watched with reverence as the perennially flowing Irrawaddy dawdled beneath a starlit sky. The voices of the *pongyis* drifting up to our pagoda platform somehow seemed to weave heaven and earth together. And a new thought arose in our Western minds. Perhaps the solutions we seek to the yet-unanswered cosmic puzzle are also no more than myths — modern ones, perhaps, but myths nonetheless.

For the pious Buddhist, the source of all knowledge is Buddhist scripture. This is as unqestionable and unchallengeable to him as empirically verified scientific facts are to western man. Eighty percent of Burma's inhabitants are Buddhist, and their description of the universe differs profoundly from the materialistic-scientific concept.

When Malunkyaputta, one of the Buddha's disciples, asked the Enlightened One about the origin of the universe, he was answered with the parable of the arrow: A man who had been hit by an arrow would not agree to have it pulled from his wound until he knew who had shot the arrow and everything about him. What did this man look like? To which caste did he belong? Where did he live? What bow had he used, and of what material was it made? Before he could get all the answers, he was dead. It is therefore futile for man to ask indeterminable questions. He should instead use his short life span to work on his salvation and to plot his course toward *nibbana*. He should strive toward the extinction of delusion, toward deliverance from all future births and thus from suffering and misery. The question of where and when the universe came into existence is unimportant, a mere game of empty words.

The universe of the Buddhist is a continuum of time, space and karma. The latter factor determines the duration of an infinite number of different worlds which rise and fall in a cyclic pattern. Within them, different layers of existence correlate with levels of insight and meditational practice. This concept seems essentially Buddhist, yet in its physical description it is not far from the modern physicist's vision of an ever-expanding universe.

But even a simplified description of this 2,500-years-old theory is difficult for the Western layman to grasp. According to the Pali scriptures, the center of the world is Mount Meru, around which circles the sun. Seven concentric ranges, separated by seven broad seas, girdle the central mountain. In the outermost sea, at the cardinal points, are the four continents, each one ringed by 500 lesser islands. To the east lies Pubbavideha, to the north Uttarakuru, to the west Aparagoyana. To the south is Jambudipa, home of men, the only continent where Buddhas are born, the only continent which allows karma to gather, and therefore the only one to offer an escape from the endless cycle of existence, from the wheel of *samsara*.

The labels are unfamiliar, but the Western mind can envision this horizontal concept. It exists within the continuum of space and time. But now comes the hard part: an additional, vertical stratum to a so-far physical world. The surface of Jambudipa is only one plane; the full gamut of human existence encompasses 31 different levels. A Burman will tell you that being born on this plane, as *homo sapiens* in Jambudipa, is the best of all possible births.

The power of one's karma — of good or evil deeds in past existences — is responsible for his rebirth in the abodes of the gods, as man on Jambudipa, or in one of the many hells. There are three clearly distinguishable realms: Kama Loka, the lower world of sensual pleasure and desire; Rupa Loka, the middle realm of fine material being; and Arupa Loka, the upper realm of formlessness. Each is subdivided into different levels.

The higher realms — the *brahma* world — can be reached by humans through *jhanic* meditation. The deeper the meditation and the insight, the higher the level on which one will be reborn. Arupa Loka comprises the realms of infinite space, of unlimited consciousness, of nothingness, and the realm of neither perception nor non-perception. Being reborn on one of these planes does not constitute or lead to *nibbana*; it is an incorporeal existence of intellectual bliss which lasts longer than the world itself. Later, the inhabitants of this abode will be reborn in another Jambudipa, where they can again begin to develop and collect enough insight and karma to achieve *nibbana*.

The realm of Rupa Loka, the *deva* world, which lies beneath the sphere of formlessness, is subdivided into 16 sections. The beings who live here are free of *rupa* or desire, free of the senses of taste, smell and touch. They are not without form, but the higher the level, the finer the material of which they consist. They do not need food and are born without needing parents. To be reborn here or in Arupa Loka, mere good deeds are not enough: only intensive meditational practice will suffice. The 20 divisions of Rupa and Arupa Loka are attainable only for a very few. They are a goal for people who spend their life in meditation, for monks who do not have to care for their material existence, who are fed by the lay people.

For the ordinary Burman, the man who toils the soil, who has a family and who procreates, the life — even in different existences — is believed to take place within the realm of Kama Loka, dominated by sensuous desire and thought. Beings in this realm have six senses, including the sense of mental impression. They live on 11 different levels which reflect their past good or evil behavior. This realm of Kama Loka is the real world of the Buddhist, for it is here that he lives through his happiness and his sorrows.

The Burman perceives not only the concrete physical world around him; Kama Loka in all of its forms, from the deep Avici hell to the highest abode of the gods, is real to him. All the myths of Burma's ancient culture have left their marks in this realm. Pre-Buddhist concepts of the world as well as animistic, Brahmanical, astrological and alchemistic ideas found their respective niches in this cosmic construct — which, despite its diverse and colorful appearance, is nevertheless a world of ethics and morals, of reward and punishment.

The lowest abodes of Kama Loka are the different hells. The punishments which await those reborn there are even more horrible than those described by the medieval Christian church. There are eight grades of hells — some dark, some cold, some hot, and some causing eternal pain. Just as the bliss of gods continues for immeasurable time, so does the punishment of hell. Perhaps the most wicked of all deeds which causes a person to be banished into this abyss is the wilful murder of a monk, an action so heinous that even good karmic deeds cannot compensate it.

Above the hells comes the animal kingdom. Rebirth as an animal is regarded as a severe punishment, even though animals live close to men, beneath, on and above the surface of Jambudipa. The Jataka stories, the Buddhist fables which tell about the Buddha's former lives, often depict the future Exalted One as an animal — but as an animal who could do good, collect good karma, and so move upwards to higher and more rewarding levels of existence. The life span of most animals is too short to allow them much chance to perform meritorious deeds; thus, they depend on human beings to share their merits with them. It will take a long time until these animals are reborn again as men.

Above the kingdom of the animals is the world of *pretas*, of ghosts and spectres who haunt funeral pyres and graveyards. The next level is the world of the *asuras*, or demons. They share this world with men but are seldom visible.

Next, in this system of merit-bound vertical planes of existence, comes man. He is the master of Jambudipa, the continent named after the mythical rose-apple tree which grows at its very end. Though life on this level is full of *annica*, of misery and sorrow, it nevertheless offers the only chance to escape from the eternal wheel of *samsara* into *nibbana*. Due to man's median position between the gods and the hells, between happinesss and sorrow, he and only he is able to advance by the nature of his meritorious deeds. If his meditational insight permits, he can perhaps become a "stream enterer" who will be reborn in one of the higher planes of existence. He could even become a "non-returner," one who will be reborn in the heaven of the effortless gods and find his way directly to *nibbana*.

The inhabitants of the other three continents surrounding Mount Meru live in continuous bliss and therefore have no chance to do good. But Buddhism concedes something like free will to the man of Jambudipa. This free will cannot influence man's present condition, which has been predetermined by former lives. But it can be directed toward his future incarnations , those he can influence by living according to the Dhamma, the Buddha's law. This law can be accepted on different levels. For the simple peasant it is enough to follow the five basic precepts. If he doesn't kill, doesn't steal, doesn't lie, has no unlawful sexual intercourse, and abstains from intoxicants, he can be sure that a similar or better life will wait for him. For *samaneras*, novices to the Sangha religious order, and for *pongyis*, or monks, there are an additional 222 rules which regulate a life geared to higher wisdom and deliverance.

Though still a part of Kama Loka, the Deva Lokas — abodes of the gods — come next. Their location is on the foot, on the slopes, on top of and above Mount Meru. These Buddhist gods, a remnant of pre-Buddhist Brahman cosmology, are not omnipotent beings. They are mortals, just as human beings are. But their life spans, consisting of continuous sensual bliss, are immensely longer than those of humans; what's more, these gods have extra physical and psychic powers. That man but seldom gets a glimpse of them is understandable. Their time continuum is so very different that a lifetime to man might be measured in minutes by the gods.

There are six Deva Lokas above the sphere of human misery. These include the abode of the Four Rulers of the Cardinal Points, the Thirty-three Gods, the Yama Gods, the Tusita Gods, the Gods of Nirmanaratis, and the Parinirmita-vasarvatin Gods. Highest of all gods and the ruler of Kama Loka is Mara. He is the personification of sense-desire, the instigator of sensual bliss, the god of evil, the symbol of everything the Buddha has surmounted. Man's existence is torn between the power of Mara and the Law of the Buddha. The mundane satisfaction of the senses keeps man in Mara's claws, feeds him with short-lived sensations, and punishes him with sorrow. Those who do not follow the path of the Buddha, those who cannot escape into *nibbana*, will always remain pawns of Mara. They will traverse Kama Loka between the hells and the heavens for an indeterminably long time.

The belief in such a world, in a cosmology which has changed only marginally five centuries before christ, is surely not universal among modern Burmese Buddhists. Progressives and liberals have interpreted many cosmological "facts" as only symbolic, but orthodox Theravadins still believe in the literal scriptures as the ancients did. They know that to give in, to reinterpret meanings which for millennia were based on a common understanding, would spell the end of Theravada Buddhism. Similar pressures in the last millenium caused Buddhists in India to give in to the Hindu interpretation of the world and to reinterpret scriptures which until then were of a commonly understood nature. Mahayana Buddhism as a result underwent profound change. The orthodox Theravadin refuses to change; to him, the world interpretation of the western physicist is just one of many cosmologies on the periphery of the Dhamma, of the true law.

Today, Burmese state schools which teach Newton's law are gradually replacing the *pongyi-kyaung*, the old monastery school prevalent in Upper Burma. But it will be a long time before a purely physical cosmos is accepted. For the Burmese, the complex unity of Kama Loka, where the karmic power of man is one of the structural elements of the universe, is much more beautiful than what modern science tells him. And how could it seem unreal when the words of the Lord Buddha made it understandable to everybody? body?

And.ª Bernieri dis. inc.

Kium,

astéro

ARIMADDANA

The Dawn of a Nation

Shortly after the historic day in 1044 A.D. when Anawrahta's mythical spear, Areindama, pierced the body of his half-brother Sokkate and made him king over the 19 villages in the plain of Pagan, a yellow-clad recluse by the name of Shin Arahan was brought into the new ruler's presence. This Buddhist monk, son of an Indian Brahman in Thaton, turned Anawrahta's mind toward a religion which was breathing its last in India, where it was being routed by the steady and merciless advance of Islam.

Anawrahta was what modern political scientists would call a nation builder, master of an art of statesmanship which is given only to a few. He knew that if he wanted to reign over more than just a few villages as his forefathers had done, he had to become the promoter of a unifying belief, the protector of a common ideal which would bind people together.

The "11 villages of Kyaukse" were his economic mainstay. Though situated in the dry plain of Upper Burma, they were watered by four ancient rivers and a system of artificial irrigation that had been in use there since time immemorial. This plain of Kyaukse produced enough surplus paddy (rice) to feed not only the royal household but also artisans, monks and soldiers without whom Arimaddana — as Pagan was then known — would never have outgrown its original tribal structure.

Shin Arahan, the pious eremite monk (whose sculpted features can still be seen today in the Ananda Temple), introduced Anawrahta to the conservative interpretation of a philosophy which, during its 1,500-years existence, had been proven to plant sense and commitment into the hearts of its followers. It was this event which brought Burmese history to a turning point. Buddhism provided the long-sought superstructure needed to create a superior culture, and marked the Pagan era as one of humanity's most brilliant periods.

Anawrahta had his challenge. His ideal was the 3rd Century B.C. Indian empire of the Mauryan King Ashoka, the outstanding example of success by a Buddhist "universal monarch." It was Anawrahta's aim to become such a "universal monarch," to be the benevolent ruler who cared for his people, who guarded the Dhamma, and who brought peace and prosperity to Jambudipa. The king concentrated all his faculties toward achieving no less than that. Shin Arahan's entreaties for a set of the Tipitake scriptures also gave Anawrahta reason to go to war. He fought the Mon empire in southern Burma, wrestled the sacred palm-leaf scriptures from the hands of the Thaton king, and simultaneously molded people of different racial and cultural backgrounds into one nation.

In the 800 years since Anawrahta's reign, Buddhism has been the unifying theme enabling Burma to survive centuries of war and migration. Indeed, the Burmese nation exists because of Theravada Buddhism. But the converse is also true. Theravada Buddhism might not exist at all today were it not for the Burmese. During the 11th Century, Southern Buddhism's last stronghold in Sri Lanka was threatened by a Chola Hindu invasion. Burma's material support, and the valid ordination of Ceylonese monks by their Burmese brethren, turned the tide against the Cholas and made a vulnerable creed survive a most perilous time.

The first centuries of this millennium, the years during which Pagan flourished, were also the crowning years for other Southeast Asian kingdoms. In the Indonesian archipelago, Srivijaya, a wealthy Indianized state, held a virtual trade monopoly on all goods which passed from the east to Arabia. In the Khmer empire, Suryavarman II, a contemporary of Burma's Kyanzittha, oversaw the building of Angkor Vat, Southeast Asia's greatest single religious monument. This was the time when the seed of Indian culture, planted in foreign soil, came into full bloom. Vaishnavism, Shaivism and Mahayana Buddhism, sometimes blended together, fathered the timeless beauty of Southeast Asia's religious sculpture and architecture.

In Burma, these Indian craftsmen — whose handwriting can also be traced at Borobudur, Angkor Vat and Angkor Thom — came in whole guilds. Some were refugees from the advancing Islamic forces; others came as regular contracted workers to help build the temples of Pagan.

The inhabitants of Burma's Arakan and Ramanadesa coasts already had long-standing relations with the Indian subcontinent. Traders and Brahman priests had settled at the river mouths in the first centuries A.D., and it was through them that Theravada Buddhism established its first foothold on the mainland of Southeast Asia.

Further north, the earliest influence came from Sanskrit Buddhism, from the Mahayana and Tantra variants of this world-shaking creed. But these interpretations were not embedded in the hearts of the people and lacked the rigorous adherence to scriptural order found in the Theravada. By the time Anawrahta came to power, religious decadence had set in. It is no wonder that the captured Thaton king, Manuha, saw the Burmans as just a barbaric tribe from the northern wastelands, without any valuable culture.

That changed within a generation. Mon scripture, Mon architecture and the more cosmopolitan lifestyle of the coastal people took root at Pagan. It took hold largely because Anawrahta had 30,000 Mons — artisans, monks and traders —transferred to the capital of his once land-locked kingdom.

More than just one charismatic leader was required to solidify what was to become a multiracial nation. History endowed Burma with two more kings within a century whose deeds fit the description of "universal monarchs": Kyanzittha and his grandson Alaungsithu. Together with Anawrahta they were the founding fathers of a Buddhist nation the equal of Ashoka's legendary kingdom. For 250 years, Arimaddana strutted its greatness.

The temples of Pagan, though today only 2,200 remain of a former 13,000, have over the centuries been a lasting inspiration to the Burmese people. They serve not only as reminders of the Dhamma, the timeless Buddhist law; they also tell of a bygone glory, one which installed a cultural continuity that survived Mongol, Shan, Chinese, British and Japanese invasions of the country. Inscriptions which survived eight centuries of heat and rain tell us that the aim of life during Pagan's epoch of brilliance was not personal enrichment. The law of Karma, which led man to earn merit by endowments and donations, was the foremost ethic principle. An air of constant striving for goodness lay over that era.

Though the king was virtually lord over his subjects' life and death, he was no god-king and was himself bound to the Dhamma. He depended on his advisers and on acceptance by the Sangha, the fraternity of monks. Oriental despotism, as 19th Century European scholars called this system of government, takes on a very different aspect under a benevolent ruler. In times of chaos, he offered the only possible way to amass men and material for the fight against enemies and natural forces.

For simple peasants in remote villages and for monks in their monasteries, life already had a democratic character. Elders and elected representatives of village councils, and the total equality which ruled the order of monks, were the counterbalance to an otherwise oppressive time.

The chronicles report the wrongdoing of certain of the rulers. But they also tell how these men came to inglorious ends. Most kings not only promoted Buddhism; they constructed their personal lives as examples for the faithful. Thus we can envisage Alaungsithu when he said:
"May I always be conscious and aware
Of kindness done to me!
Union of ill friends be far from me!
Beholding the distress of men and
deathless gods,
I would put forth mine energies
And save men, spirits, gods,
From seas of endless change!"
For a king to express such feelings is not common in human history. But in Burma, Alaungsithu was not alone. Other rulers also left inscriptions which showed their yearning for *nibbana* and their profound belief in a world where gods, *nats*, men and ghosts lived together — but where only men could earn merit and share it with the other beings of the universe.

When the temples of Pagan were built, the light
of the Dhamma rose over the country.

More than 2,200 buildings, all constructed to
improve karma, are strewn without apparent
design all over the plain of Pagan.

Now we shall tell the story of Pagan Arimaddana.
When the Lord revealed himself, he passed in his
journeyings from the Middle Country and came to
the site of that kingdom. He stood on the summit
of Mt. Tangyi, and looked and saw a white heron
and a black crow alight on the top of a bueta tree
on a steep bank; moreover he saw a preta in the
form of a monitor with a double tongue abiding
with the fork of the bueta tree, and a small
frog crouching at its base. And he smiled. His
cousin Shin Ananda entreated him saying, 'Why
smilest thou?' And the Lord prophesied and said,
'Beloved Ananda! In the 651st year after my
parinirvana there shall be a great kingdom in
this place.'

The Glass Palace Chronicle of the Kings of Burma Part III, 113.

Contrary to the lofty halls of contemporaneous
Gothic cathedrals, the interiors of Mon-style
temples are narrow, cool and dim: ideal places
for meditation.

Just as it was during the time of the temple
builders, thanaka bark powder is the universal
cosmetic for Burmese beauties.

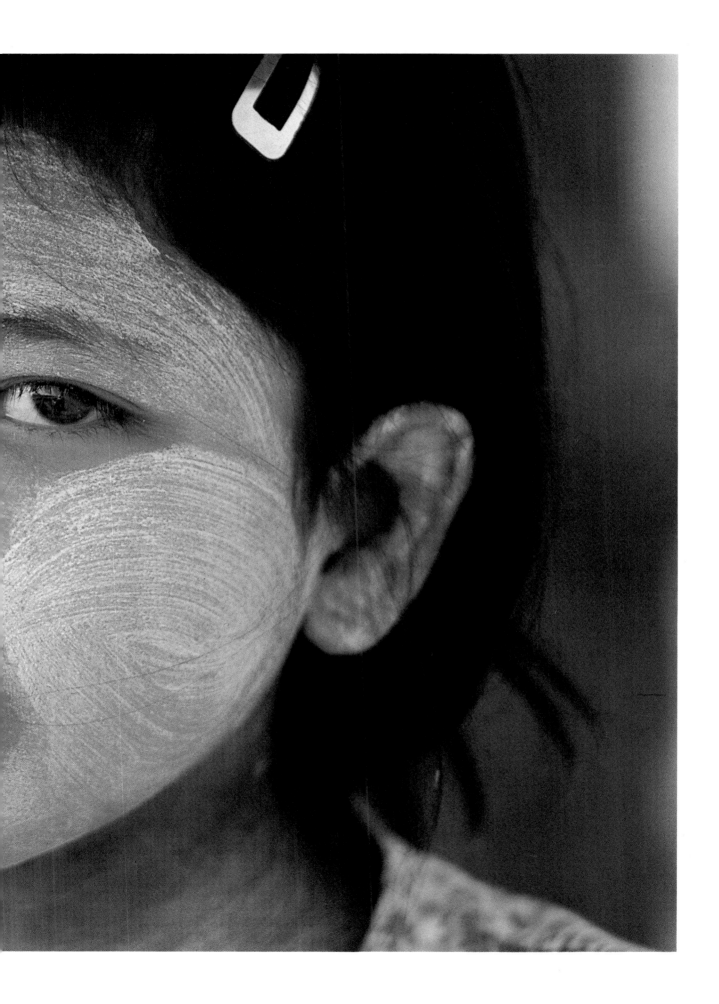

For 800 years, Burmese have bowed for protection and blessing under the bended arms of the Ananda Buddha.

This realm of Pagan is so named
because it is the fairest and dearest of lands.
It is called Arimaddana
because its people are warriors
who vanquish their foes,
and even its name is terrible.
Its folk are free from pain or danger,
they are skilled in every art,
they possess the tools of every craft,
they are wealthy,
the revenues are past telling
and the land is full of useful things.

Verily it is a land more to be desired
than the Himavanta, the fairy land.
It is a glorious realm
and its people are famed
for their splendour and power.

Tun Nyein, Inscriptions of Pagan, Pinya and Ava Monastery inscription 1343 A.D.

". . . their getting aged, becoming toothless, gray haired and wrinkled, the failing of their vital force, the wearing out of their senses; this is called decay."

Abidhamma Pitaka

One day eight noble saints stood for alms
at the king's palace. And the king took
the bowl and fed them with food, and asked,
'Whence come ye?' And they said, 'From
Mt. Gandhamadana.' Now king Htihlaingshin
was full of faith, and he built and offered
the saints a monastery for the rainy season.
He invited them to the palace and fed them
with food continually during the three month of rain.
Once he entreated them to call up by their
power the likeness of Nandamula grotto on
Mt. Gandhamadana. And they did so. And king
Htihlaingshin made a great gu after the
likeness of Nandamula grotto, and called
it Nanda.

The Glass Palace Chronicle of the Kings of Burma Part IV, 140/3

Reminiscent of the snow-covered peaks of the
Himalaya, the white spires of the Ananda Temple jut above the hot and arid plain of Pagan.

For 250 years, between the 11th and 13th centuries, nearly every king and minister had a temple,
stupa or monastery built for the perpetual glory
of the Tathagata and their own karma.

Today, peanut fields are found where the cross-roads of an empire once converged.

Two temples, two lifestyles: the Ananda points
skyward in its cosmopolitan Mon style, while the
weighty Thatbyinnyu reveals the still earthbound
soul of the upland Burman.

Every single ancient building of Pagan is also a
monument to the Indian heritage of Burmese
culture.

Then the Blessed One addressed
the brethren, and said,
'Behold now, brethren, I exhort you,
saying, "Decay is inherent
in all component things!
Work out your salvation with diligence!"
This was the last word of the Tathâgata!

The Maha Parinibbana Sutta, Chap. VI, § 10.

A dying Buddha, constructed by a vanquished king, intimates a yearning for deliverance from the wheel of samsara.

The mighty Dhammayangyi has nothing of the sublimity of the Ananda, upon which it was based, but it shows the finest masonry on the plain of Pagan.

Today, as during the heyday of Pagan, the weather-beaten Burmese peasant is the indestructible backbone of the nation.

MANDALAY

The Base of the Burmans

During the 9th Century A.D., an uncivilized tribe emerged from the gorges of the southbound Himalayan rivers. When they stood at the fringe of the hills, clad only in their tattoos and bark loincloths, with the torrid plain of Upper Burma and the malaria-infested river mouths in front of them, one of humanity's longest migrations was about to come to an end.

For nearly 2,000 years, these tribesmen had migrated from Gansu in northwestern China, via the source of the Yellow River in northeastern Tibet, through Yunnan and over the mountains of northwest Burma down to the rice-growing plain in the vicinity of today's Mandalay.

Chinese records from the latter half of the second millennium B.C. tell of the Ch'iang, a race of shepherds and goatherds who inhabited the loess plateau to the west of the Han Chinese homeland. They were the ancestors of the modern Burmans. Their culture at that time seems to have been as developed as the Chinese: they already used bronze vessels and tools. The pattern of their painted pottery can still be traced on modern Burmese earthenware.

But sheep transform meadows into wasteland where cattle cannot graze, and the Chinese expansionists were cattle growers. The Ch'iang had to choose between submission and migration. They opted for the latter without knowing what hardship it would bring to future generations, until they finally came to settle in the Irrawaddy River basin.

During their 2,000-year migration, the Ch'iang lost most of their ancient cultural traits. They had to trek over mountains, through deserts and jungles; they became nomads, jungle dwellers and hill people. What was lost of their original Neolithic culture, they substituted with more adequate techniques of survival. They learned to hunt, to fight and to breed horses. They became experts with the bow and arrow. Perhaps most important of all, they developed some immunity to tropical fevers and sores. When they stood at the edge of the mountains and were about to descend into the blistering heat of the lowlands, one could still have called them barbarians without being far wrong. So it is astonishing to find these people at the core of Southeast Asian history within only two centuries of their primal contact with the Indianized culture of the coast.

In the Irrawaddy valley, the new arrivals found a land already irrigated by the Mons, a people who had entered the country 1,000 years earlier through the valley of the Salween. Here on the Kyaukse Plain, four rivers — the Samon, Panlaung, Zawgyi and Myitnge — provided a year round water supply to the flat land beneath the Shan Mountains. In this fertile basin, the Burmans established their first settlements. Subsequent dynasties built their capitals here. The first was Pagan, followed by Sagaing, Ava, Amarapura and Mandalay. History has proved the uniqueness of their choice. From the sites of their respective capitals, the royal courts were able to manage the economy by controlling the main waterways.

To travel today by boat from Pagan up the Irrawaddy, passing the mighty confluence with the Chindwin and then turning toward the east, one still can see the remnants of ancient power centers strung along the river banks like pearls on a string. There is Sagaing with its myriad temples, pagodas and monasteries, stretching along the northern embankment where the only bridge spans the Irrawaddy. Directly opposite, on an artificial island at the mouth of the Myitnge River, the ruins of Ava mark the site of the city from which the Burmans controlled the country for the longest period of time. The 20-odd kilometers from Ava to Mandalay are dotted with religious remnants built during the Konbaung dynasty period when the kings resided here, at Amarapura. This short stretch along the Irrawaddy can be thought of as Burma's heart. Here Burmans and Shans wrestled for centuries to dominate the land; here, after a defeat by the Mons in the 18th century, the renewal of Burman hegemony began.

In 1852, after the Second Anglo-Burmese War, the British occupied all of Lower Burma. The Kingdom of Ava, as Burma then was known, again became a landlocked state. This seclusion made it easy prey for British colonial aggression. The revolutionizing ideas which had swept over other parts of Southeast Asia in preceding centuries had little contact with and less effect upon Ava, where the court exhibited an ostentatious lifestyle only marginally different to that of Kyanzittha's 12th Century court.

King Mindon, the founder of Mandalay, ascended the throne during the Second Anglo-Burmese War. Even though he was more modernistic than his predecessors, he tried to inspire a sense of national unity by ceaselessly propagating the ancient Buddhist ideals. His "Golden City" of Mandalay was built upon a pattern which included archaic Brahmanist symbols and maxims. The Fifth Buddhist Synod, which Mindon convened in this city, symbolized the king's intent to make Mandalay the center of the universe and — following the Buddha's personal prophecy — the

"New Jerusalem" of the Buddhist faith and Burmese renewal.

But this was no obstacle to British firepower. In 1885, they came up the Irrawaddy and against only minimal resistance, occupied the new capital. They sent Mindon's son, King Theebaw, and his queen, Supyalat, into exile in India, where they vanishd from the pages of history, and with them the Burmese monarchy.

For a decade the British had to fight against local guerillas, who even without central coordination made the hill tracts and villages of Upper Burma ungovernable for the viceroy's administration. Then, as it had done time and again when the country was in a period of ebb, Upper Burma produced the men and ideas to secure the continuity of the indigenous Burmese culture. Once Western ideas, technology and weapons had demonstrated their unquestionable superiority, alien influences were incorporated into that unique mixture which became modern Burmese culture. Today, this culture — an amalgam of Buddhist conservativism and social progressiveness — has no comparison on earth.

The occult remains an important part of life in this far-off region. Be it the Nat Festival at Taungbyon, some 32 kilometers from Mandalay, where every August a multitude of people meet to worship two of the 37 national *nats*; or be it the palmists, astrologers, soothsayers and tattooers who populate the stairways of Mandalay Hill; numerous indicators of archaic influences are very visible. Neither Buddhist nor Western scientific, they are basically animistic remnants of a past preserved in much greater depth than meets the casual eye.

One can also recognize the Indian heritage wherever Buddhism has its strongholds. One such place is Sagaing, the former capital which today is a village of 600 monasteries and 5,000 monks. It is Burma's foremost retreat for persons who want to renounce the world, and for those seeking a quiet valley in which to meditate. Sagaing is also the place where families of standing in Upper Burma send their sons to be accepted into the Sangha, to follow the path of Buddha and his son Rahula. Here the boys undergo their *shin-pyu*, their initiation ceremony, the first step in a man's life toward *nibbana*. As long as this ceremony continues to be performed on nearly every young Burman, there is no fear that the old Burmese values will vanish. Every young man who starts his adult life with weeks of meditation in the hills of Sagaing will be imbued with the incomparable beauty inherent in the original Burmese way of life.

The world's largest book is contained in 729 temples, each covering a marble-hewn page of the Buddhist scriptures.

Hereditary slaves were once dedicated to the temples. Many of their descendants still do the same job voluntarily. They feel they are bound to the law of their karma.

In front of the pagoda,
with ruffled mein,
his head raised,
his chest up,
his tail upturned,
as if about to roar
or leap forward,
so proud
the brick lion
looks.

One day
on his back
the droppings of birds,
those banyan seeds,
broke into the brick,
up a plant sprouted;
the roaring proud
lion
still keeps his haughty mein.

Mg Tha Noe

Chinthes, mighty mythical lions, guard the entrances to sacred grounds.

Sweeping a temple is sweet karmic food for a Burmese. . . .

....so is the artful execution of the Buddha's image.

The cheroot is as much part of the true Burmese,
as the cup of tea is of the English.

A boy's riches may be in his heart as well as in his smile.

Sanda Moke Khit, once an ogress who cut off her breasts in reverence to the Buddha, later was reborn as King Mindon, founder of Mandalay.

Especially during the evening hours, when the
land is engulfed in the light of the setting sun,
Burma truly becomes the Golden.

All that is left of what was once the "Golden City
of Mandalay," the center of the universe, are the
battlements. . . . .

. . . while most of the sacred buildings beyond the
walls survived the savagery of the Second World
War.

Tongas trudge along the dusty roads of Upper Burma.

When they were all assembled, the Lord Omniscient
thus addressed the image of himself:
"I shall pass into Nirvana in my eightieth year,"
he said,
"but you, instinct with my essence,
will live the five thousand years
which I have prescribed for the duration of the Religion."

The Maha Muni prophecy, Sappadanapakarana

Mandalay's Maha Muni is a place where mystic
moods meet and mix.

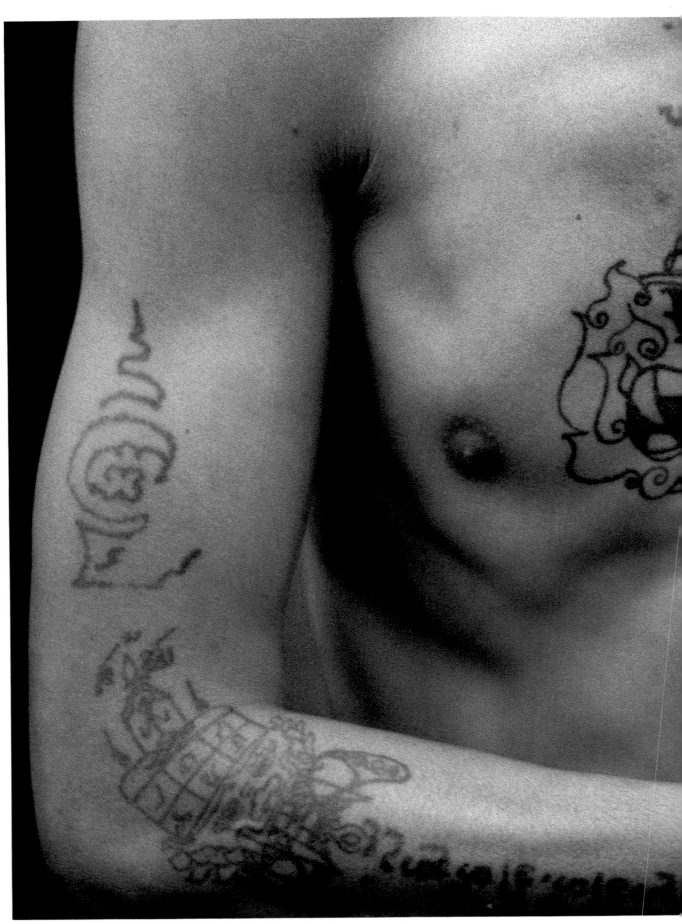

As recently as the 1930s, some Burmese national-
ists still valued tattoos as an invulnerable shield
against British bullets. They paid a heavy price.

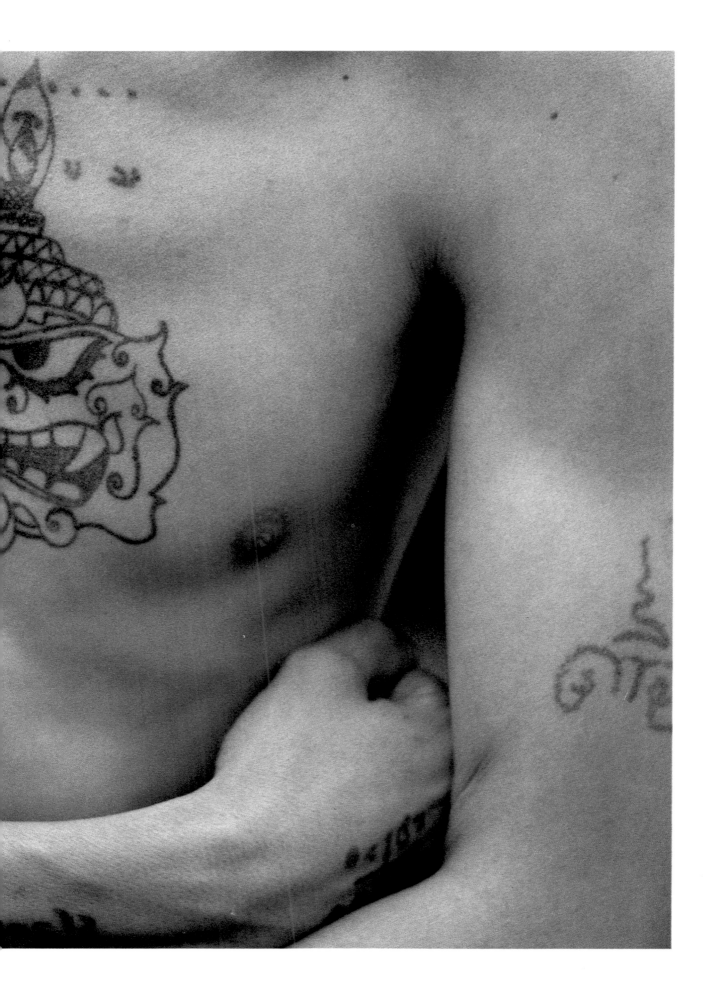

Occultism is a perpetual part of the Burman's daily life. Next to the astrologer, the palmist is regarded as the best person to look into the future.

What rational Buddhism cannot accomplish for
the believer, nats can. People turn to them in
times of distress.

O Lord of the sunrise and sunset.
O Hsa Seing Lung, with brush and flag,
with paper chain, with bunches of golden flowers,
with food and drink,
I humbly make offering to you.
It has happened to me this day
that I have vomited my food and my drink.
I have not been able to sleep
and only with difficulty have I been able to eat.
O Lord make the heat of my body subside,
let eating be pleasant
and my fever depart.
O Lord, I shiko to you,
this day I worship you.
Give me shade and shelter;
let me have shade, let me have shelter.
O Lord I beseech you.
From now, henceforth,
let me continue to live happily
with my father and mother, with my son and wife.
Lord! There is none other like you.
Let me remain peaceful and prosperous.
Let my life be firm as a rock
and compact as a roll of leaves.
Please return now to your abode,
O Lord,
I humbly shiko to you.

Samong Hpon, A Nat Invocation

Nats are not only nature spirits. Inhabitants of
celestial abodes, they often represent historical
persons.

The temple-dotted hills of Sagaing are a sacred
Burmese landscape.

"In him, bikkhus, who has calmness of the mind, the restlessness-and-worry that has not arisen does not arise, the restlessness-and worry that has already arisen is abandoned."

Ninth Sutta, Anguttara Nikaya

A luminous alabaster Buddha radiates contemplative compassion.

Glossy and dark and soft and curly is his hair,
spotless and fair as the sun is his forehead;
Well proportioned and prominent and delicate is his nose;
Around him is diffused a network of rays.
The Lion among Men!

Buddhist Birth Stories

It is hard to turn away from the Enlightened One
at the U Min Thonze Pagoda.

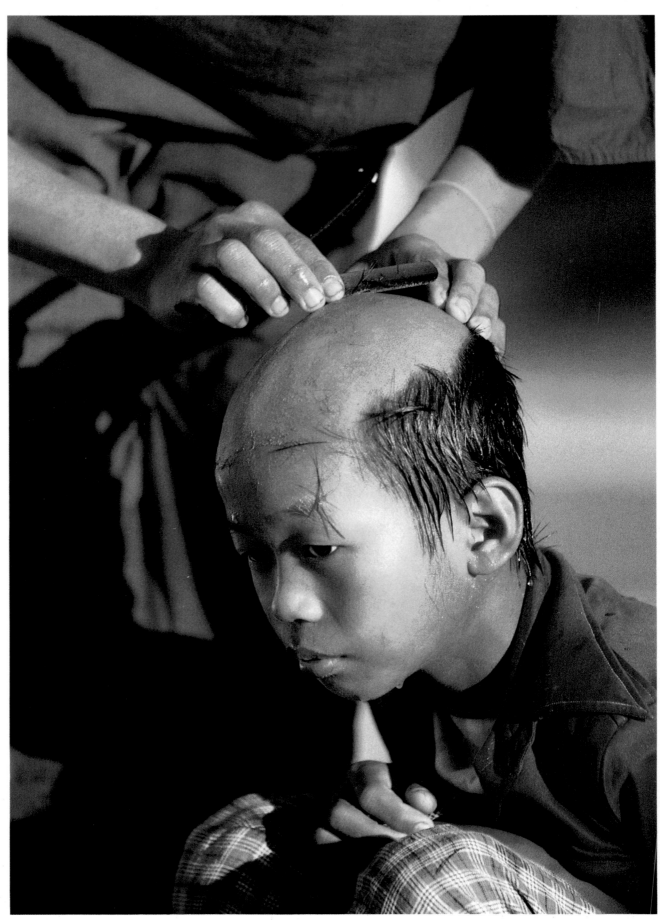

"These are mere filth as regards color, shape, smell and location. These are not I, not mine, not a soul or a being, but are impermanent, a cause of suffering and not self."

The Blessed One turned the boy not back.
And the people with the Blessed One,
                were not able to stop him.
And so he went with the Blessed One
                even up to the grove.
Then the Blessed One thought:
"This wealth, this property of his father's,
                which he is asking for,
                perishes in the using,
                and brings vexation with it!
I will give him the sevenfold Ariyan wealth
which I obtained under the Bo-tree,
and make him the heir of a spiritual inheritance!
                And he said to Sariputta:
"Well then do thou, Sariputta,
                receive Rahula into the Order."

The Buddha takes his son into the Order. The Story of the Lineage.

"Reverend Sir, may you be pleased to give me
the robe, and out of compassion for me, may you
initiate me as a novice so that I may be able to
overcome all the suffering in the round of rebirths and attain nibbana."

"Reverend Sir, I ask for initiation in order to enable me to escape from the trouble of samsara. For the second time, Reverend Sir, I ask for initiation. For the third time, Reverend Sir, I ask for initiation."

"The three robes, and the alms bowl,
Razor, needle, and girdle,
And a water strainer: these eight
Are the wealth of the monk devout."

The Story of the Lineage.

Fully invested as a samanera he turns away from
his family. . . . .

. . . and takes his place amidst his pious peers.

ARAKAN

Vestiges of India

Burma is divided into three distinctly different zones which also function as ethnic watersheds. The Mountain ranges in the east, running south from the mighty Himalaya to the Isthmus of Kra, are the home of mostly non-Burman hilltribes. The Irrawaddy River basin and the alluvial plain in Burma's center are to a great extent peopled by the Burmans themself. Clearly divided by the hills of the Arakan Yoma to the west lies the fertile coastal strip of Arakan.

The people who live here, on the offshore islands and along the eastern coast of the Bay of Bengal, are of a most peculiar mixture. Undoubtedly of Mongoloid extraction, they have so much Indian blood in their veins that their very features bear witness to the land's turbulent history — a past which reflects Arakan's vulnerable location between antagonistic races and religions.

In times long past, this was a Hindu land. The first immigrants, from Bengal and Bihar, were Indians who brought to Arakan the same factors of cultural and religious evolution that had changed their homelands. It was a time of Brahmanical resurgence, a time in which the old Vedic religion was reinstated in its new Hindu look. Buddhism, which had spread over most of India in the centuries before Christ, survived — but in its Mahayanist form, it was often indistinguishable from Hinduism.

Chronicles record a line of kings reaching back to the year 2666 B.C. More certain is the kingdom of Dhannavati, which flourished at the beginning of the Christian era. In this erstwhile realm, the sacred Maha Muni image — the guardian of Arakan's independence — still stood as late as 1784. Dhannavati was succeeded by Vesali, a kingdom which drew its name from a legendary Licchavi city in India. The last of the ancient Arakanese kingdoms, it vanished during the Mongolian invasion of 957 A.D.

All of a sudden, Arakan changed. The invading tribes made the country face east, away from India. As Burma began to flex its muscles, the profound changes born at Pagan started to transform Arakan. The Tibeto-Burmans who had entered the country had come to stay. So had Theravada Buddhism, which reached Arakan via Ceylon, South India and South Burman.

Legend tells us that the Maha Muni image of the Buddha is as old as the faith itself. Certainly, it made north Arakan a Holy Land for Buddhists. Pilgrims from all over Southeast Asia flocked to the old site of Dhannavati. They came to worship an image for which, it was said, the Omniscient One himself stood as model.

Over the centuries the physiognomy of the Arakanese people changed. The racial mixture of Indo-Europeans with the only recently arrived Central Asians became predominantly Mongoloid, an ethnic mixture which still characterizes today's Arakanese.

The five centuries which followed the arrival of the Tibeto-Burmans in Arakan were an age of darkness. Arakan became a powerless tributary of Pagan and Ava. It was only after the country turned toward the west again during the 15th Century that a cultural renaissance began, inspiring the heyday of Arakan's history.

By the 13th Century, Islam had conquered the hearts and souls of the people between Africa's Atlantic seaboard and Bengal. It disseminated the most powerful set of values of the age. Not unexpectedly, the Buddhist kingdom of Arakan drew its new life through the aid and assistance of the Islamic ruler of Gaur. This Bengali sovereign in 1430 reinstated King Narameikhla to his rightful throne: 24 years earlier, Narameikhla had been ousted by the Ava Dynasty. He had spent the intermediary years at the Gaur court learning revolutionary ideas in the fields of mathematics and natural sciences, which together with monotheistic belief had fostered the Islamic success. Asia's feudal caste-oriented societies could offer no lasting resistance, and were unable to halt the eastward surge of this formidable alliance of faith and knowledge.

Arakan was to profit from it all. Contrary to the Burmese kingdom, it welcomed the new perspectives. From the Portuguese, who appeared in the coastal waters during the 16th Century, the Arakanese acquired the art of seafaring. Within only a short time, the whole coast from Chittagong to Pegu was under their control. They traded with the Lusitanians, the Danish and the Dutch, and until 1666 they bravely withstood the mighty Moghul Empire from which they had snatched the southern part of Bengal. Reports from that period paint a fantastic picture of a world full of magic and miracles, of splendor and grandeur.

But surely that was only one side of the coin. The seafaring Arakanese, together with the Portuguese half-castes who had settled south of Chittagong, were also known as Maghs. They were a race of pirates and slave traders who terrorized the peaceful population of the Ganges Delta region.

It was also during this time that the sad story of Shah Shuja came to its tragic climax at Mrauk-U, Arakan's splendid capital. Shuja was the rightful heir to the Moghul throne but was cheated and defeated by his vicious brother Aurangzeb. Sandathudamma, the king of Arakan, granted him asylum; this benevolent gesture, however, was only meant to deceive Shuja. In fact, Sandathudamma was after the Shah's beautiful daughter and the immeasurable treasures he carried. When Shuja, in whose eyes the Arakanese king was only a Magh warlord, refused to give his daughter in marriage, he and his retinue were cold-bloodedly slaughtered. Shuja's daughters ended up in Sandathudamma's harem, but when the king was unable to break their Moghul pride, they were killed within a year.

Throughout these centuries of power, Brahman astrologers and runic scientists protected Arakan with the medieval magical art of *yadaya*. Its purpose was to put the hidden powers of the micro and macrocosmos at their disposal. They accomplished this with incantations and bells, which — ringing at astronomically predetermined times and places — drove frightened enemies from the country, made kings invincible, and protected the land from natural disasters.

Buddhist cosmology, medieval Islamic sciences and ancient Brahman rituals gave 17th Century Arakan its unique character. The mood of the time, the exotic setting of the place, were unprecedented in human history. If today we imagine Arakan as it was then, we must not cast judgment on ethics and morality. Instead, we must glance with wonder at an intriguing and fascinating era which received the seed of its magic-ridden peculiarity from the clash and cross-fertilization of opposing cultures. Indeed, the magic of *yadaya* was so powerful that it was only by adopting incantations and magic ritual to their own purposes that the Burmans put an end to Arakan's invulnerability in 1784. Once the sacred Maha Muni had been dismantled and carried over the Arakan Yoma to Amarapura, where it was to fulfill the same portentous magic for the kings of Burma, Arakan's history as an independent kingdom came to an end.

In 1824, when the British annexed Arakan during the First Anglo-Burmese War, Arakan's doors were flung wide open toward India, as they had been over 1,000 years earlier. During the subsequent colonial period, landless immigrants from Bengal came and settled freely in the country. Many of them stayed after Burma's independence, transforming the ethnic and political landscape of the province.

There is still some enmity between the Burmese and the Arakanese, though in the final analysis they speak the same language, profess the same religion, and live similar lives. The real antagonism in today's Arakan exists between the many pure-blooded Bengalis, who constitute the bulk of the Muslim citizenry, and the Tibeto-Burman Buddhist majority.

As secluded as Arakan is today, connected with the outside world only via Rangoon, it looks east again. But this time, it is a set of Western ideas which penetrate from that direction. For it is socialist democracy which now bings new life to this magical province at the end of the world.

Morning mist envelops a Myohaung monastery.

Indra, the former Vedic god, has gone through many metamorphoses. In Buddhist India, he became Sakka; in Burma, Thagyamin.

"Ye dhamma hetuprabhava . . .
The Buddha hath the causes told
of all things springing from causes;
And also how things cease to be,
'tis this the Mighty Monk proclaims."

The Buddhist creed.

The matchless Maha Muni, once venerated as the
palladium of independent Arakan, is thought to
be as old as the Buddhist faith itself.

Arakan's sacred architecture is strikingly diffe-
rent from the way temples were built in the
Burmese kingdoms. An example is this 19th
Century shrine in Akyab. . . .

... and the famous Shitthaung temple-refuge
constructed during the 17th Century.

A multitude of creeks, rivers and canals act as
Arakan's predominant transportation arteries.

High-wheeled ox carts trail dust and mud behind
them as they ramble around the villages.

As you ask me where I live,
Full description I will give.
A vendors stall and spirit shrine
Mark the dwelling which is mine.
Stands in front a banyan tree
With altar-work of masonry.
At the back in solid mass,
Tube-rose and lemon grass.
Lie to south of where I dwell,
Onion patch and water well.
To the north in serried row,
Spice and bulbs of ginger grow.

Maung Myint Thein

Peaceful living persists in a forgotten corner of
the world.

In Arakan, small and inexpensive gadgets still
enhance the beauty of the people.

Mountaintops and ridges teem with picturesque
pagodas. . .

... while forgotten Gautama images are hidden
in the hills.

Before the fog fades, the undulating countryside
of Arakan reveals its fairy-tale features.

Arakan's coast yawns at the mouth of the Kala-
dan River.

A coastal sailing craft enters the Lemro river.

And the crystal disc of the sun,
The shining solar wheel,
Spills its light to stream through the sky
Dazzling the world,
While the glass studded palace of gold sends back
Its spreading rays in wondrous mingling
To reach the very center of the sky:
A sight of endless joy.
Thither I raise my suppliant hands;
And when I go to rest I reverently pay homage,
And thither I turn my gaze
When I wake from sleep.

Let-we Thon-dara (1764)

Another day fades away on the Bay of Bengal,
where the world proverbially ends.

The nat living in this launggyet tree will never
have to move as long as the inhabitants of the
area continue to bow to him in reverence.

INLE

Inthas, Shans and 100 Tribes

Every year, during the Burmese month of Thadingyut, the southern Shan State hosts a unique championship. Participants are young men from the 200 villages fringing Inle Lake, Burma's most picturesque body of fresh water. These Intha tribesmen compete in a "leg-rowing" regatta: their eel-like boats must be propelled by the power of their leg muscles only.

The Inthas are a tribe of 70,000 who originally lived in the Tavoy region of Tenasserim. Their own tradition tells that they began migrating to this lake district as early as the 14th Century. Most probably they only completed their resettlement at Inle during the 18th Century, when their homeland was ravaged by the continuous wars between the Siamese and the Burmans.

The Inthas' story is a picture-book example of human adaptability, of man's ability to survive in the face of seemingly unsurmountable odds. This theme is as topical today in the mountains of Burma as it was a thousand years ago. The Inthas' success story is one of a very few. When they left their Tavoyan homeland as a small tribe and resettled in this far-off mountain region, they had to acquire a totally new set of cultural survival techniques.

The men became fisherman whose unparalleled way of rowing their boats and whose unique conical fish traps are to be found nowhere else in this world. Their wives' floating gardens are equally unique. Since the land fronting the lake belonged to the Shans — the original inhabitants of this area — when the Inthas arrived, the immigrants had to move *on top* of the lake. There they constructed their own gardens on the water. They matted dried reeds, covered them with muck scooped from the lake bottom, and anchored these two-by-100-meter floating gardens around their stilt houses with bamboo poles in the shallow lake. Today the Inthas are Burma's foremost vegetable growers and flower gardeners.

Their prosperity is in stark contrast to the conditions under which most other small hill tribes live. Burma's ethnic composition, as in all of Southeast Asia, displays traits of the universal human struggle for better land and better living conditions which every generation tries to produce for its offsprings. Migrations, tribal conflicts, regional upheavals and civil wars are part and parcel of daily life between the Himalayas and the South China Sea.

The only solution offered in today's world to relieve this turmoil is the creation of strong central governments. But none of the countries in this region has yet succeeded at accomplishing that. In Burma, part of the problem lies in the fact that the central government is in the hands of the Burmans, the country's dominant race and the group which controls the best land. On them an enlightened solution depends.

The geographical distribution of Burma's tribes is a perfect example of the natural law by which the best land goes to the strongest people. The irrigated plain of Upper Burma and the Irrawaddy River valley are inhabited by the Burmans. They also share the coastal area and the prime rice-growing region of the Irrawaddy Delta with the Mons and the low-land Karens. After the Second World War, this land was all but confiscated by the Chettyars, a caste of South Indian money lenders who understood nothing about growing rice but knew perfectly well how capitalism works. The Burmans reacted with a coup d'etat which drove the Indians out of Burma and gave way to a redistribution of land to the dominant groups.

Continuous pressure comes today from the people who still live in the hills. They too know the value of a land "where a mere tickling of the ground answers with a golden harvest," as George Scott once commented. A migratory trend toward the more fertile lower elevations is still taking place: a group of Karens has settled in the fertile Delta region which was only opened to cultivation during the British period. But most of the non-Burman peoples are still entrenched in the hills.

The largest single minority group is the Shans, whose 3.2 million people constitute the second largest ethnic group in Burma. The Burmans know what that means. After the fall of Pagan, the Shans — whose name in Chinese means "mountain people" — came down from the hills and tried to dislocate the Burmans from their new-found homeland. The struggle went on for centuries, and even though the Shans had the upper hand in the beginning, the Burmans finally succeeded in repossessing the fertile fields of Upper Burma. One subdivision of the Shans had more luck: they moved down the Menam valley on the other side of the mountains dividing Burma and Thailand, settled amidst the Mon-Khmer speaking inhabitants of the region, and founded the Siamese nation.

In Burma, the Shans had to settle on the undulating eastern plateau and along the river valleys which cut through the mountains. Until a few decades ago, they were split into 34 feudal principalities, each one headed by a hereditary prince — a so-called *sawbwa* — who ruled in medieval fashion. Like the Burmans, the Shans are Buddhists.

Around them, settled on mountain slopes and ridges, live a conglomerate of tribes who are mostly animists, spirit and ancestor worshippers. They compose the third and poorest stratum of Burma's manifold races.

Some 126 ethnically or culturally distinct groups inhabit the Union of Burma. The most numerous of them — the Shans, Karens, Mons, Kachins, Chins and Arakanese — all have their own state, and according to the 1974 constitution, a certain autonomy. They also have clandestine armies which are in perpetual action, trying to break their races away from the Union and from Buman overlordship.

Most small tribes cannot show a success story like the Inthas'. Theirs is a hard and burdensome life. Their crops don't just grow by "tickling the earth;" rice, maize, millet, buckwheat, beans, sesame and cotton must be grown by slash-and-burn agriculture, one of the most work-intensive methods of planting cereals and vegetables. Once a piece of virgin forest has been chosen as future cropland, the trees are felled and burned. The fields are then plowed, harrowed and sown, with ashes fertilizing the ground shortly before the monsoonal rains break. Even with scientific crop rotation, these fields are depleted after three or four years. Then a new piece of land must be cleared since the now-exhausted soil needs at least 10 to 12 years to recuperate. Fields therefore must be moved further and further away from the dwellings, until finally the village itself is moved to a more central location.

The Was, Akhas, Lahus and Padaungs are typical of the small tribes who cannot leave their mountaintop homes since all arable land in the lower regions is already occupied. They are in a perennial fight for survival, less a confrontation of man against man than a struggle of man against nature. Though tribal families have an average of seven children, only 40 percent of them survive, infancy. That is already more than the meager soil can feed. They are caught in a vicious circle. They have to shorten the time their fields lie fallow and this causes the harvest to diminish with each year.

It is no wonder they search for new ways to feed their growing populations. They have profited most from the planting of a cash crop in such great demand that it earns enough money for the tribesmen to buy food at the marketplace. This cash crop is poppy, more specifically, the tears of the poppy, also called *papaver somniferum* or opium.

By observing the hill country of eastern and northern Burma, one can see why some tribes developed into strong nations while others remained stagnant for centuries. The forces of history are today in northeast Burma as they were during the Neolithic age. But then there were few people and a seemingly limitless world. Today, there is little arable land available, and the population continues to grow. The Burmans and the Shans were the last of the tribes to find their "promised land," some 800 to 1,000 years ago. Their growth, from small tribes to large nations is definitely beyond the reach of the inhabitants of the remote mountains.

A floating garden and an Intha leg rower exemplify the ingenious adaptability hill tribes have developed during their centuries of migration.

The depth of Inle Lake does not exceed three
meters. Inthas employ special techniques in
fishing here.

Birth after birth, over and again,
With dirt and besmirching,
Oppression and evil,
Fading and withering,
Longing and craving,
Crying and groaning,
Clutching and clinging,
Panting and gasping,
Sobbing and weeping,
Toil and weariness,
All pervading round and round
Like a spinning wheel.

Ko-gan Pyo

The daily fight for survival has left its mark on the faces of many slash-and-burn cultivators of the hills.

The Inthas of Inle Lake migrated from the
Tenasserim region to find a tranquil and prosperous new life.

Cheroots. . . .

. . . are still made by hand.

Pregnancy cannot be caused by many men;
the child is his at the time of whose intercourse
the three causes combined,
and the three causes are the proper season of the woman,
copulation with a man,
the release of a fate by the death of some animal . . .
The fate may be released
from any being in the animal kingdom,
a human being for example,
and in its fast orbit around the earth
it searches for a new home which will be
where the woman in season combines with the man
and where the fate is fated to come to rest.

Law and Custom in Burma and the Burmese Family.
The Buddhist's view on procreation.

The Pa-o of the southern Shan State are of Karen
stock and speak a Tibeto-Burman language.

It is a burden being big brother. . .

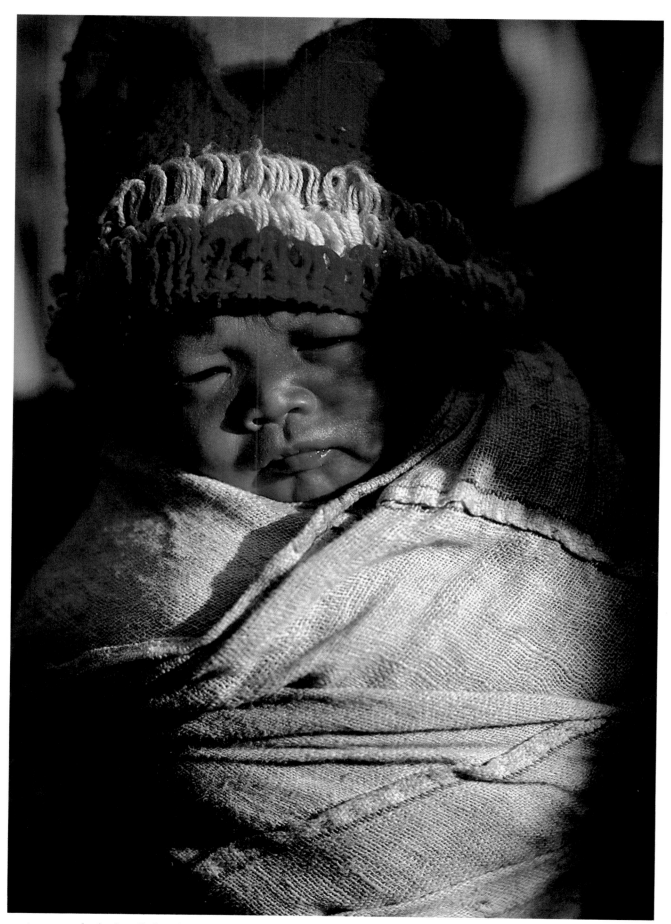

... to an apathetic, bundled-up baby.

The Shans are the majority race in the hills. They
are closely related to the Thais on the other side
of the border.

The towel is the Shans' turban.

Once she has reached a certain age, a woman is
expected to wear only black dresses.

The shifting market which comes every fifth day
to Taunggyi is a feast of food and fun. Members
of most of the hilltribes are found in attendance.

Curry and chillies are condiments for the peasants' palates.

There is more than one way to ride a buffalo.

Before the monsoonal rains come, most houses
need new roofing.

Two lone fishermen ply their trade on Inle Lake.

The journey thru' life is not straight and smooth:
The winds and waves and storms are rough-
But let them do their worst.
The rain pours and hailstones batter,
Some small, some big-
But let them do their worst.
Come rain, come sun, come raging storm,
I am not dismayed:
I shall press on with my journey,
Wherever it takes me, rejoicing,
And singing, as I go, the sweet song of life.

The anthem of life, Tek-katho Min Maw

An Intha poles a newly acquired garden across
the lake.

A fishing fleet seems to be suspended on its own
reflection.

RAMANADESA

The Land of the Talaings

At a time when the ancestors of the Burmans had barely left their Gansu homeland, the Mons — another people from the windswept plains of Central Asia — had already reached the fertile coast along the gulfs of Siam and Martaban. Fifteen thousand years earlier, a long-forgotten race had domesticated plants and established humanity's first agricultural civilization in this region.

When the "Ramans," as the Mons called themselves, arrived in their land of destiny, they founded a kingdom which they proudly called Suvannabhumi, the "Land of Gold." This kingdom was a loose federation of three states on either side of the Tenasserim Range. In the east were Haripunjaya in what is now northern Thailand and the legendary kingdom of Dvaravati, located in the vicinity of modern Lopburi. West of the watershed lay Thaton, the ancient capital of the Burmese Mon-land.

For 1,000 years, the Mons were the unchallenged rulers of that land. They became Southeast Asia's most cultured people. The surviving art and architecture bespeak of an era of peace, prosperity and deep religious feelings. While other tribes which live today in Burma were still enveloped in a Neolithic culture, Suvannabhumi was already a part of Greater India. It shared the wisdom and social development of the Mauryan and Kushan empires on the subcontinent.

All of Southeast Asia could have become the Mons' domain. They had the knowledge and the opportunity of those who arrived first. But they were not a warrior race: they were a race of poets.

Suvannabhumi was a Buddhist kingdom. The oldest written Buddhist records speak of two merchant brothers from Okkala, a village in the kingdom of Thaton, who offered Gautama Buddha his first meal after the seven-week-long meditation which followed his enlightenment. In exchange for this kindness, they received eight hairs of the Exalted One. They carried them to their ruler King Okkalapa, who had a stupa built on Singuttara Hill, just above what is today Rangoon. This stupa became Buddhism's most venerated shrine, a gold-covered wonder of architecture, an edifice which incorporates everything genuinely Burmese, a place of exaltation and awe, a gilded spot in the landscape which can be seen with the naked eye from 12 kilometers aloft. This Shwedagon Pagoda is a sacred monument where kitsch and art, meditative silence and laughter, playing and praying, religion and business blend into unique Burmeseness.

In the third century B.C., the Mauryan king Ashoka sent two elders, Sona and Uttara, to Suvannabhumi to propagate the Buddhist gospel. Outside of Thaton, they built the Kelasa monastery, from which the eternal truth of the Dhamma spread throughout mainland Southeast Asia. But changes came after the middle of the first millennium A.D. when Hinduism regained dominance in India, and when Brahmans and traders, the true conveyors of Indian culture, brought Hindu and Mahayana ideas to foreign shores. Soon after the T'ang dynasty fell in China, a carousel-like migration of tribes began applying intensive pressure on the Mon people already settled along the golden coast. Within a few centuries, Thaton had fallen to the Burmans, Dvaravati to the Khmers, and Haripunjaya to the Tai-Shans.

East of the mountains, the Mons vanished as a political entity, absorbed within the Siamese and Khmer kingdoms. Not so on the Burmese side. For very soon after Anawrahta's conquest of Thaton, the conquerors were sitting at the feet of the vanquished. Among the Mons' pupils was King Kyanzittha, the very monarch who had subjugated them and established a Burman supremacy that was to last as long as the Pagan kingdom flourished. Kyanzittha favored Mon architecture; his inscriptions were all in the Mon language; and his romantic love affair with the daughter of the king of Pegu is a main theme today on Burmese stages. The Mons taught the Burmans what they themselves had learned from the Indians, and in return the pious strength of the Pagan kingdom preserved the orthodoxy of Theravada Buddhism for the Mons.

The Mons' historical mission was not yet ended. Their kingdom, the real Ramanadesa, was yet to leave its mark in the annals of Burma. Like a phoenix out of the ashes of the fall of Pagan, the Mons reappeared as rulers of a new empire.

Their capital, which they called Hamsawaddy, was known as Pegu to the Europeans who were about to set their feet on the soil of Further India. A substantial immigrant population from the Telingana coast of India called the capital Ussa, after the Indian city of Orissa. Their presence led to the inhabitants of Ramanadesa being known as Talaings, a name the Burmans liked to use because it indicated heavy Indian influence.

Ramanadesa was founded by Wareru, a Shan. The Mons didn't like him and had him put to death, but only after he had completed the Dhammathat, a law book which remains the basis of civil law in modern Burma. It converted the rulings of the ancient Indian law giver Manu into a Burmese context.

From 1287 to 1539, a 250-year period equal in length to the life span of the Pagan empire, Ramanadesa represented Burma to the outside world. This kingdom had its ups and downs, but Pegu's most glorious period was not a time of expansion and wars. Neither was it a time of dominance over other people. Instead, Pegu is remembered for a century-long era of peace and prosperity which came about not as a result of enslavement and war booty, but because of the industriousness and labor of its own people.

Shinsawbu, the beloved queen of this era, gave the Shwedagon its present form and died with her eyes fixed on the glorious golden structure. To her, it symbolized the existence of the three worlds of man, *devas* and *brahmas*. As a devout Buddhist queen, she was sure to be reborn in one of the higher celestial abodes. (After the British conquest of Lower Burma, the Mons spread the word that Queen Victoria was a new incarnation of Shinsawbu.)

She installed as her successor the most able man in the kingdom: Dhammazedi, a learned monk who was also a *Zawgyi* — an alchemist and a master of runes. He had the universal knowledge of his time. Believers in the power of runes left a lore which tells about his life.

Dhammazedi and his companion, Dhammapala, were monks who taught Shinsawbu, then a Mon princess married to the king of Ava. Shinsawbu was unhappy and flew with her two tutors back to Pegu. She later became queen, and when her life was nearing its end, she was in a dilemma over which of her two instructors should marry her daughter and become successor to the throne.

Dhammazedi was finally chosen, but Dhammapala, also a master of the runes, was envious and secretly plotting against the new king. He studied long and hard, and finally found the ultimate runes. If he could stay buried under the earth unmolested for a period of seven days, all the hidden powers of the universe would be at his disposal.

Dhammazedi who knew that his former companion was on the verge of success, had Dhammapala's apprentice tortured until his master's burial place was revealed. Virtually in the last minute before the prescribed time was completed, Dhammapala was dug up. Dhammazedi was thus able to deny him his life and supreme knowledge. Had the magician eaten a piece of the corpse he would have gained the ultimate truth himself, but Dhammazedi abstained. In later years, he rediscovered the ultimate runes himself; but he used their power only to be a righteous king, ruling in a manner which enhanced the knowledge of the Buddha's words in his kingdom.

Chronicles reveal that Dhammazedi was the king who sent monks to Sri Lanka for a valid ordination. Due to this ordination — still the backbone of today's Sangha — every young monk knows the names of his teachers' teachers, all the way back to Gautama himself.

After Dhammazedi, the decline of Ramanadesa set in. In 1539, when it was incorporated into the Second Burmese Empire, the final requiem was played for a kingdom to which the Mons of today look back in melancholy regret.

The Mons did make one attempt in the 18th Century to reclaim power. But Alaungpaya, the charismatic Burman leader from Shwebo, eliminated once and for all the dream of an independent Ramanadesa. The Mons who did not flee after the fall of Pegu were assimilated by the Burmans. It was Alaungpaya who founded Rangoon. He gave it the name "End of Strife," to commemorate the final decline of Mon power.

The predominant people of Lower Burma are the Mons. In former times, they were also called Talaings after a region on the Madras coast of India.

The old and the new, the eternal and the disposable, are seen in the face of contemporary Burma, symbolized by this Sule Pagoda Buddha.

The king accompanied by Thagyamin
went to the forest abode of Teikthadhamma,
who asked the reason for their visit.
Thagyamin said:
"As you have not long to live,
we have come to beg of you the precious relic
which was given to you by the Enlightened One.
We would build a pagoda over it
where it would always be worshipped when you are no more."
The hermit, after considering the matter for some time,
agreed to give to them the Buddha's hair
on the condition
that they found a rock of the same shape as his head.
The relic would be deposited
in the hollow of the rock,
and they could then build their pagoda over it.
Thagyamin was very pleased
and at once departed for the sea shore, where he found
a huge rock which resembled the head of the hermit.
A great number of people helped him
to drag the rock to the top of a high hill.
The hermit then took the precious relic
which was interwoven in his hair
and placed it in the hollow of the rock.
Over this hollow a new pagoda was raised,
Thagyamin returned to his celestial abode
and the hermit passed peacefully away
at the foot of the pagoda.

The Legend of the Kyaik-tiyo Pagoda

A mere handful of boys can rock the boulder, but
the crucial balance is held by a hair of the
Buddha enshrined on top.

Burma's fertile landscape of paddy fields and pagodas produce nourishment for body and soul.

An enchanting Sakyamuni meditates in the far-
off hills of the Mon-land

The sublime smile of the dying Tathagata reminds the Buddhist that he must strive for his own salvation.

More is the treasure of the Law than gems;
Sweeter than comb its sweetness; its delights
Delightful past compare. Thereby to live
Hear the five rules aright:
Kill not-for Pity's sake-and lest ye slay
The meanest thing upon its upward way.
Give freely and receive, but take from none
By greed, or force, or fraud, what is his own.
Bear not false witness, slander not nor lie;
Truth is the speech of inward purity.
Shun drugs and drinks which work the wits abuse;
Clear minds, clean bodies, need no soma juice.
Touch not thy neighbour's wife, neither commit
Sins of the flesh unlawful and unfit.

Sir Edwin Arnold, The Light of Asia

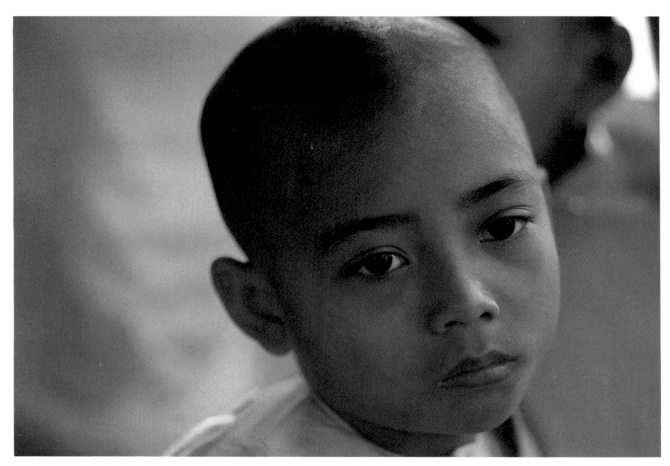

The Buddhist nun, believing in karmic reincarnation, helps others in order to help herself escape samsara. . .

. . . whereas the Catholic Sister, awaiting the day
of resurrection, in the meantime works for the
betterment of her fellow citizens.

Paddy is the principal product of the fertile fields
in the delta.

Life is peaceful where the rhythm of rice-growing
regulates the activity of the people.

The Golden Pagoda, Rangoon's Shwedagon,
looks back on a history of 2,500 years.

Pagoda spires sometimes look like radio anten-
nae set up to receive messages of an other-
worldly nature.

Covered with plates of pure gold, the Shwedagon
is not of solely spiritual value.

When Sakka opened the ruby casket
to take out the hairs to be washed,
the hairs flew up to a height of seven palm trees,
and rays of many colors
emanated from them.
The Petas could see the men,
and the men could see the ghosts.
The blind recovered their sight.
The dumb could speak.
The crippled regained their strength.
The earth and the water shook.
The Meru bent its head.
The seven ranges shook together
Sheet lightning and forked lightning played in the sky.
A rain of jewels fell.
Trees bore fruit
and flowers bore blossoms out of season.

The Founding of the Shwedagon, Shwedagon Thamaing Athit.

The washing of a Buddha image, frequently seen
at the main platform, corresponds to a meditative
soul cleansing.

An Indian-style dvarapala stands in front of one
of the innumerable tazaungs around the golden
stupa.

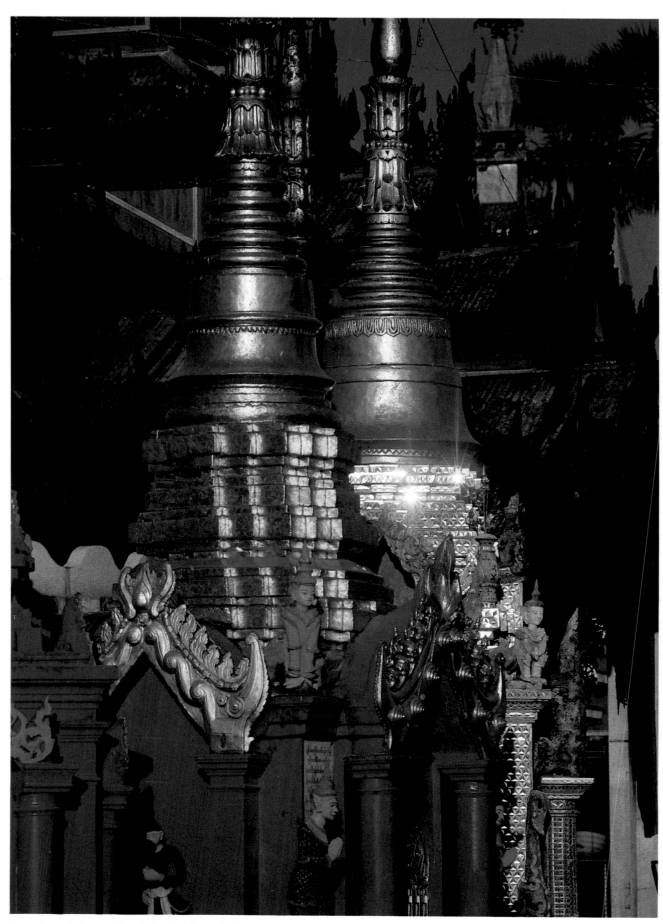

Sixty-four shrines with golden finials encircle the
octagonal base of the stupa.

Stupas, tazaungs, pyathats and tagundaings all
assist in lifting the soul of the pious toward the
infinite, the universal Dhamma.

185

To give to monks a dwelling place,
Wherein in safety and at ease
To think and insight gain
The Buddha praises most of all.
Let therefore a wise man,
Regarding his own weal,
Have pleasant monasteries built,
And lodge there learned men.
Give food to them, and drink,
And clothes, and dwelling-places
To the upright in mind.
Then they shall preach to him the Norm-
The Norm dispelling every grief-
Which Norm, when here he learns,
He sins no more,
Reaching the perfect well.

Vinaya, Chullavagga VI, 1

Even though the Shwedagon may sometimes resemble Sleeping Beauty's castle, it also produces an enduring air of meditative reflection and karma consideration.

"I take refuge in the Buddha,
I take refuge in the Dhamma,
I take refuge in the Sangha."

The Buddhist's prayer.

How transient are all component things!
Their nature's to be born and die;
Coming they go; and then is best,
When each has ceased, and all is rest!
As rivers when they fill must flow,
And reach and fill the distant main;
So surely what is given here
Will reach and bless the spirits there!
If you on earth will gladly give
Departed ghosts will gladly live!
As water poured on mountain tops
Must soon descend, and reach the plain;
So surely what is given here
Will reach and bless the spirits there!

Maha-Parinibbana-Sutta

Bo-bo-gyi, the guardian nat of the Shwedagon, is
dear to Rangoon's residents.

Flowers and faith go hand in hand for the
Buddhist.

Everywhere in the country, pongyis travel for free.

The Irrawaddy riverboats, though battered and
aged, remain a mainstay of transport.

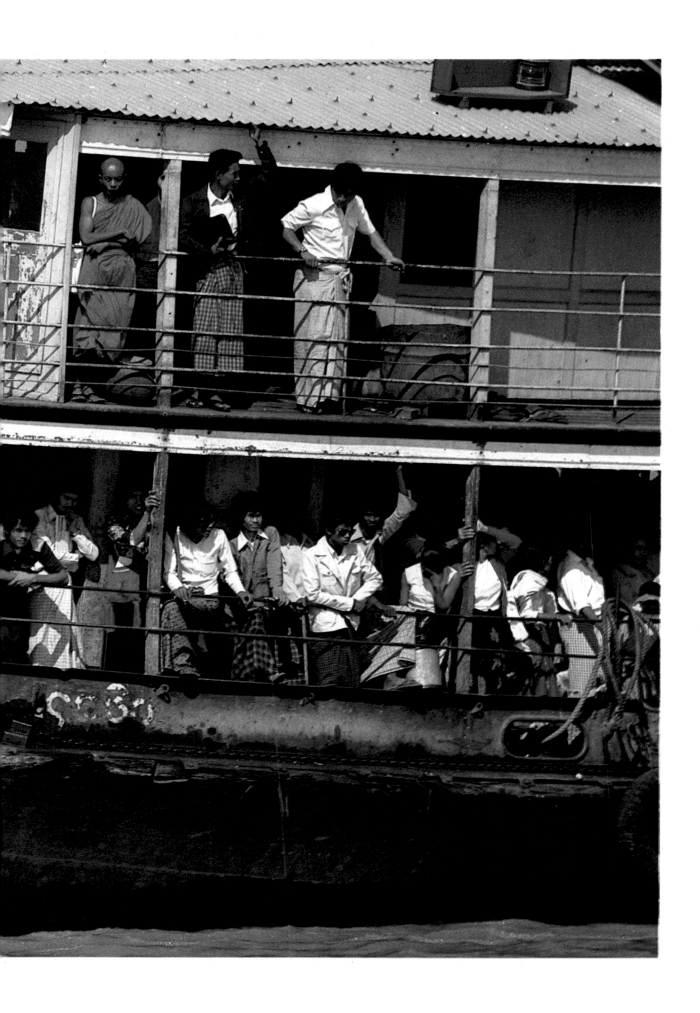

It will be our duty
to retort in no uncertain terms
that the wisdom or knowledge
that might be attributed to Karl Marx
is less than one-tenth of a particle of dust
that lies at the feet
of our great Lord Buddha.

U Nu, From Peace to Stability (1951).

In modern Rangoon, nothing has changed since
the 1930s.

Selling after-dinner treats in the open air: a cheroot and betel-nut stand. . . .

...and a sidewalk cookie kitchen.

Modern utensils are like modern ideas, stream-
lined and shiny for a faster turnover.

The Burmese never tire of watching movies.

They are a smiling race, even though they often
carry a heavy load.

If one subtracts the glory with which Buddhism envelops the country, Burma is just another under-developed nation. One cannot afford to throw away anything that might be reuseable.

All matter and mind,
according to the Law of Impermanence,
are in a constant state of change and motion,
with the old ever decaying and dying
and the new ever-rising and growing,
the whole state of flux ceaseless
ad infinitum.
In the same way the history of the human society
is also in a constant state of change;
all the material life
and the spiritual life of that society
are continuously and ceaselessly
changing and moving;
while the old social and political systems
of the history of the human society
are heading towards decay and death
the new are in the process of birth and evolution;
the Law of Constant Change is ever determining
the history of the human society.

The System of Correlation of Man and his Environment (1963)

Many delta rice mills like this one are run,
maintained and owned by Chinese families.

Rangoon's port is the principal gateway to the
outside world for an otherwise-isolated nation.

SOCIALIST BURMA

A Transitory Present

History tends to repeat itself. The changeover from Buddhist tenets to socialist principles, as political maxims for government action, follows a well established pattern in the history of Burma. In 1059, Anawrahta of Pagan commenced the building of the Shwezigon Pagoda by constructing a shed for the images of the 37 Nats, the religious protagonists of their time. The king expected the people who came to worship the *nats* to be slowly won over to Buddhism, converted to a radically different but more enlightened vision of the world.

It was a time of profound change and cultural awakening. Present-day Burma is in a similar state of transition — a state of crisis in its traditional culture, where foreign ideas, again of a universal character, must be adapted to Burma's complex socio-historic fabric.

Even though Burmese socialism is based on Marxist thought, its main emphasis is on the word "Burmese." Just as Buddhism had to shed its orthodox character to incorporate Burma's traditional spirit worship, so the tenets of Burmese socialism are forced to encompass a good many Buddhist strains.

There are a number of philosophical grounds on which, it would seem, a sufficiently broad base could be laid for Buddhist-Marxist syncretism. The Buddhist precept of constant change, the impermanence of all existence, is not unlike the Marxist idea of permanent revolution and on the Hegelian principle of thesis, antithesis and synthesis. Their common rejection of the theory of creation, their denial of the existence of a soul and of an omnipotent god, and their mutual belief in a primeval utopia of communal property which vanished only with the advent of individualism and selfishness — these are common territory.

U Nu, the first prime minister of the Union after its independence, tried hard at first to reconcile the two philosophies. He regarded the social philosophy of Marx as part of the lower sphere of human endeavor, adequate for attaining "Lokka Nibbana," the *nibbana* within this world. Buddhism was at a superior plane where the yearning for spiritual liberation, which Marxism is unable to satisfy, could be answered and fulfilled.

Soon, just as Western socialists had predicted, the incompatibility of the two philosophies surfaced. Fundamental Buddhist belief in the existence of spiritual beings, the doctrine of rebirth within the wheel of *samsara*, and the acceptance of Karma — the predetermined reason for present conditions — had no place in socialist doctrine. Vice versa, the basic theme of socialism, that man has the ability to direct his own destiny, had no place even in an adapted Buddhism.

U Nu's medievalism was in a stark contrast to the modern scientific approach necessary for solving the problems of an emerging nation whose traditional culture was being challenged. Once during the 1950s, when political and military pressure from the minorities' secessionist struggle was mounting, Nu had 60,000 sand pagodas built all over the country to propitate the *nats* and thereby ward off danger for the nation.

U Nu's government called itself socialist. Nonetheless, he convened the Sixth Buddhist Synod in Rangoon, a deed which in the eyes of the Buddhist majority made him a future Buddha. This symbolism supported his anticommunist propaganda campaign which made clear to everybody that orthodox Marxism, with its Western materialistic world outlook, was incompatible with the ancient values alive in the country. U Nu won the 1960 election with religious revivalism on his banner, and a promise to make Buddhism the state religion.

A group of military officers, heroes of the struggle for independence, had more realistic perspectives. Their basic concern was the inherent inability of traditional Burmese culture to compete on an equal level with an aggressive world economy. U Nu's election brought this progressive faction to the forefront. They ousted the Buddhist premier in a coup in 1962, proclaimed the "Burmese Way to Socialism," and tried to steer a course halfway between Marxism and Buddhism, with a focus on secular and pragmatic politics.

"The Systems of Correlation of Man and His Environments," which outlines the official ideology, is seen by orthodox Western socialists as just one of many "socialist" doctrines which appeared in Third World countries during their post-independence years. These Westerners feel the

"Burmese Way" misses the clear-cut rationality of scientific materialism. But it is nevertheless a major step for a people whose basic values are 2,500 years old and have not changed within the last millennium. U Chit Hlaing, the probable author of the treatise, employed the traditional expository style of the Pali scriptures to explain the theory of material development. This theory is alien to the Burmese mind, trained since childhood in the Buddhist dogma of impermanence and unreality. As the Visuddhi Maggha states:

"Mere suffering exists, no sufferer is found;
The deeds are, but no doer of the deeds is there;
Nirvana is, but not the man that enters it;
The path is, but no traveller on it is seen."

The task faced by the Revolutionary Council was similar to that of Anawrahta some 900 years earlier. To instigate a profound cultural change, there could be no violent opposition to the ancient belief. The national leaders had to give way to more modern and pragmatic attitudes in a slow and convincing manner.

The basic Buddhist tenet of karma is still the major philosophical obstacle between present-day Burma and a socialist society. Although, on one hand, belief in predetermined causes for present conditions worked as indigenous legitimation for the power held by the Revolutionary Council, it also kept the Burmese from challenging a government which came to power by a coup d'etat.

Now it is more than 20 years after Burma shut its doors to the outside world, two decades after the propagation of the Burmese Way to Socialism and the creation of a legitimately elected one-party government. Now it is the young generation, the men and women who grew up after 1962, on whom future events will depend. They have attended youth camps and political seminars, but they also have gone through their Buddhist initiation ceremonies. The influence of traditional values remains especially dominant on the village level, where the government tries not to interfere.

But the Sangha is not so immune to interference. The still-powerful brotherhood of the monks has significant political influence on the people. Twice since 1962 the government has tried to purge political opponents from the ranks of the holy order by demanding registration and purification. This is an act with many historical precedents. The kings of old, who styled themselves as protectors of the Sangha and defenders of the faith, used the same pressure to keep the Sangha from becoming too strong.

Burma has been unified four times. Anawrahta, Bayinnaung, Alaungpaya and Aung San are the respective heroes of its history. The last one; Aung San, who was barely 32 years old when he was assassinated in 1947, belonged to the same generation as the present leaders of the country. They have now reached old age and tend to be more open to compromise with each passing year. Their legitimation came from their successful fight against British and Japanese imperialism.

This is a legitimation which the now-emerging young leaders do not have. Their experience is on the administrative level, gained during the years of nation-building which are now coming to a close. Hopefully, this experience has instilled in them the pragmatism they dearly require to solve the enormous economic, racial and cultural problems still haunting the country.

Burma is one of the handful of countries in today's world where the power of myth is still visible in everyday life. The struggle of Burma's people, individually and collectively, to lead meaningful lives in an universally accepted context of precepts and laws, will go on and will probably never end. It will make every period of history transitory, an idea on which Buddhism and Marxism deeply agree.

Burmese are marching into a future which might
be markedly different from the past.

This modern Burmese girl is unwilling to concede
that "religion is opium for the people."

A socialist functionary in traditional Burmese dress, blends the new and old with a certain charm.

The Revolutionary Council of the Union of Burma
does not believe
that man will be set free from social evils
as long as pernicious economic systems exist
in which man exploits man
and lives on the fat of such appropriation.
The Council believes it to be possible
only when exploitation of man by man
is brought to an end
and a socialist economy based on justice
is established.
Only then can all people,
irrespective of race and religion,
be emancipated from all social evils
and set free from anxieties over food,
clothing and shelter,
and from inability to resist evil.
For an empty stomach is not conductive
to wholesome morality,
as the Burmese saying goes;
only then can an affluent stage of social development
be reached and all people
be happy and healthy in mind and body.

Our belief, Point One of the Burmese Way to Socialism (1962)

Otherworldliness. . .

. . . and progress now!

Today's monks might yesterday have been members of the Socialist Programme Party's youth chapter.

It cannot be that man has only now
acquired very high intellectual faculties
and developed civilisation.
Looking back on the life span of the world
and its changes we can say
that man has possibly attained,
time and again,
levels of civilisation much higher
than those of our times.
It is probable that the conditions
that had developed and become similar to those
available now must have come to ruin
on account of a certain catastrophe
which must have taken place in the whole world.
All arts and sciences, all records, all machineries
and nuclear instruments and such
must have then come to rack and ruin,
and those men who survived must have retrograded.
into the dark ages. . . . .
We like to take as fables
what we read about wonderful feats of engineering
in ancient literature, but it is possible that these feats
must have once been actually achieved,
and men must have spoken about them
and hence these fables must have come to be handed down
from generation to generation. . .
Things in this universe are transient
and every period in its life is all too brief.

The Socialist Programmes Party's interpretation of history.
The System of Correlation of Man and his Environment (1963)

The state stresses physical fitness for modern Burmese. For the Buddhist, the body is only a temporary shell to be discarded along the path of samsara.

The drummer...

...and the paraders resemble American high
school marching bands and contrast strikingly to
the monochrome of similar groups in other Third
World socialist countries.

Following the watchwords given 25 centuries
ago....

. . .and announcing the watchwords of the day.

By this abundant merit I desire
Here nor hereafter no angelic pomp
    Of Brahmâs, Sûras, Mâras; nor the state
And splendour of a king; nay, nor the steps
    Sublime of pupils of the Conqueror.
But I would make my body a bridge athwart
        The river of Samsâra, and all folk
Would speed across thereby until they reach
    The Blessed City. I myself would cross
And drag the drowning over. Ay, myself
    Tamed, I would tame the wilful; comforted,
Comfort the timid; wakened, wake the asleep;
    Cooled, cool the burning; freed, set free the bound.
Tranquil, and led by the good doctrines, I
    Would hatred calm. The three immoral states,
Greed, Hate, Delusion – rooted all in self –
    O may they die, whenever born in me!...

King Alaungsithu's Shwegugyi Pagoda Inscription (1131 A.D.)

For a man to work during his life-time for
the welfare of fellow citizens, for
that of the majority and for that of
man in brotherhood is indeed a beautitude.
The Burmese Way to Socialism is the
Programme of Beautitudes for the Society in the Union of Burma.
We shall constantly try our best to
make the ideology and programme of
the Party more and more entire. We
shall constantly endeavour by criti-
cal review to cleanse them of errors.
We shall constantly apply our minds to improve them.
Thus alone shall we leave to the fu-
ture generations of the society in
Burma worthy environments for their
heritage.

The System of Correlation of Man and his Environment (The philosophy of the Burma Socialist Programme Party). 1963

The social function of the pongyi is to transmit
the Buddhist way of life from generation to
generation, irrespective of political trends.

The light of the Dhamma continues to illuminate
the isolated land along the Irrawaddy, even as it
shines less and less in surrounding countries.

INDEX